24 HOURS
That Changed the World

for Youth

24 HOURS
That Changed the World

FOR YOUTH

Jason Gant

ABINGDON PRESS
NASHVILLE

24 HOURS THAT CHANGED THE WORLD (FOR YOUTH)

This book is printed on acid-free paper.

ISBN 9781426714320

10 11 12 13 14 15 16 17 18 19—10 9 8 7 6 5 4 3 2 1
MANUFACTURED IN THE UNITED STATES OF AMERICA

Contents

✝

Introduction

✝

Although Jesus was in his early thirties when he died on a cross outside Jerusalem, the authors of the four Gospels focused almost entirely on the final three years of his life. And all four Gospels devote several chapters to a single day: the day on which Jesus was betrayed, tried, and crucified. Each of the Gospel writers understood that this 24-hour period changed the world, and this world-changing day is the focal point of all four biblical accounts of Jesus' life.

A lot happened during these fateful 24 hours. From Thursday evening after sunset to late Friday afternoon, Jesus would eat the Last Supper with his disciples, pray in the Garden of Gethsemane, be betrayed and deserted by his friends and closest followers, be convicted of blasphemy by the high priest and other authorities, be tried by the Roman governor Pontius Pilate for insurrection, be sentenced to death, be tortured at the hands of Roman soldiers, be crucified, die, and be buried.

The Bible's story of redemption reaches its climax with Jesus' suffering, death, and resurrection. These events show us that God, in Christ, is literally willing to die to rescue us from sin and is more powerful than death.

The Purpose of This Study

This 7-session study for teens is inspired by and based on Adam Hamilton's popular book *24 Hours That Changed the World*. This study, like the book that inspired it, aims to give you a better idea of what went on during the final 24 hours of Jesus' life, to explain the significance of Jesus' suffering and death, and to help you apply what you learn to your day-to-day life.

Also Available

- *24 Hours That Changed the World,* by Adam Hamilton (ISBN 9780687465552)
- *24 Hours That Changed the World Video Journey,* including a leader guide by Mark Price (ISBN 9780687659708)
- *24 Hours That Changed the World: 40 Days of Reflection,* a devotional companion (ISBN 9781426700316)

Although this resource is intended for teens, the book itself is set up like an adult Bible study. Whether a leader or a participant, everyone has the same book and literally is on the same page. Leaders should review the material in advance to determine which activities and discussion questions the group will use.

24 Hours That Changed the World, Youth Edition, includes seven sessions, making it ideal for the season of Lent (one session for each Sunday during Lent, plus one session for Easter Sunday). But the impact of the hours leading up to Jesus' death is not limited to a certain time of year. Regardless of the season, this study is a great way for youth Sunday school classes or Bible study groups to get a better understanding of what Jesus and his closest followers experienced during these fateful 24 hours and what their experiences teach us about how to live as Christians today.

Each of the seven sessions includes the following parts:

Getting Started—Each session identifies a few goals for that session. These goals give leaders some clear teaching objectives and participants something to focus on as they walk with Jesus through Jerusalem. Each session also provides definitions of key words and place-names that may be unfamiliar to many participants.

Introduction—While few people have known suffering, anguish, anxiety, or betrayal on the level that Jesus and his followers faced toward the end of Holy Week, we can still draw from our experiences to get a better sense of what they felt. Every session's introduction makes a connection between an event in the hours leading up to Jesus' crucifixion and a situation that most young people today are familiar with (such as the first day of school or the night before a big test). Participants can read the introduction prior to each session or groups can spend time reading during each session.

Biblical Foundation—The best accounts of the 24 hours leading up to Jesus' crucifixion and burial are found in the four biblical Gospels. So the foundation of each session is a text from one of the four Gospels that tells the story of an event from Jesus' final hours.

Video Presentation and Discussion—An optional, but recommended resource, Adam Hamilton's *24 Hours That Changed the World Video Journey* takes viewers to the Holy Land, where he visits sites in and around Jerusalem that are traditionally associated with the events of the final day before Jesus' death. Each of the segments is about 10 minutes. Each session provides a list of sights (what viewers will see) and key insights (what viewers should take away) for that session's video segment. The session also gives a list of discussion questions that groups can use to debrief the video.

Book Study and Discussion—This part of the session is also optional. Because this study is based on Adam Hamilton's *24 Hours That Changed the World*, participants would benefit from reading and reflecting on that book. Every chapter in the book corresponds to a session in this study, and each session provides questions for groups wanting to discuss and debrief what they have read.

Bringing the Scripture to My Life—One of the main objectives of this study is to help participants make connections between the events surrounding Jesus' trial and death and their lives today. This part of each session provides discussion questions that help participants make these connections.

Going Deeper in Truth—While the biblical foundation of every session is one of the Gospels accounts of Jesus' final day, other Scriptures give us insight into the significance of Jesus' suffering and death and what we can learn from these events.

Experience Life in Community—Jesus and his closest followers were a tight-knit community. They traveled together, ate together, learned together, and forgave one another. Jesus' followers throughout history have maintained this emphasis on community, and life in community is an important part of each session.

Making It Personal—Belonging to a community of believers is an essential part of the Christian life, but the Gospel also as an impact on us as individuals. Every session gives individual participants instructions for putting what they've learned into action in the coming week.

Closing: Listening for God—Every session concludes with a time of prayer and reflection, lifting up what the participants have learned and asking God's guidance as everyone goes forth.

Session 1: The Last Supper

†

Getting Started

Goals for This Session

—Get a sense of the excitement, wonder, and anxiety the disciples felt during the time leading up to the Last Supper.

—Understand that Holy Communion is an opportunity for us, as individuals and as a community of faith, to connect with Jesus Christ.

—Recognize God's rescuing love and the importance of being part of a Christian community.

Words to Know

Seder: *Seder* is a Hebrew word that literally means "order," "procedure," or "sequence." Most commonly, *seder* is used to refer to the Passover Seder, a ceremonial meal in which Jews celebrate and tell the story of the Israelites' escape from slavery in Egypt.

Eucharist: *Eucharist* is a Greek word that literally means "thanksgiving." For Christians, *Eucharist* refers to the sacrament of Holy Communion.

Introduction: The Last Supper and the First Day of School

✝

Y ou know the feeling you get as you get ready for the first day of school? Excitement and fear set in. Hope and doubt stew in your heart. Questions like these fill your mind:

- What will my teachers be like?
- Where will I sit at lunch?
- What am I going to wear?
- Will I get lost trying to find my classes?
- Do I have the right supplies for each class?
- Which teacher will require us to sit alphabetically?
- Will I be able to work things out so that I can sit by that special someone?
- What extracurricular activities will I sign up for?
- When is the big homecoming game?
- What kind of image do I want to project to others about who I am?

Jesus' disciples had similar feelings of excitement, wonder, and anxiety as they approached the Passover feast in Jerusalem. Passover was always a big deal, a great time of year—hundreds and hundreds of people gathering to join in celebration and community, remembering what it means to be God's chosen people. It was a time to offer gratitude to God for rescuing their ancestors from slavery—even from death—under Pharaoh's rule. During the festival, they would reflect on the sacrificial lamb, whose blood was placed above the doors of Hebrew homes so that those homes would be "passed over" by the spirit of death.

It was at this moment, amid the excitement and tradition, that Jesus chose to bring to light the difficult truth of what was to come. It was the moment when Jesus invited those closest to him, his friends, to prepare themselves to understand his purpose:

> "For this reason the meal had special meaning to the disciples; they were convinced that Jesus was the Messiah and they were in Jerusalem on this Passover so he could claim his kingdom." (Adam Hamilton, *24 Hours That Saved the World,* page 15)

They were anxious to hear what Jesus would say. They may have formed in their minds what it would be like, probably even dreamed about it, much in the same way we anticipate the first day of school:

- What will Jesus do to show his power?
- Will Jesus bring down the ungodly in an instant?
- What will Jesus ask of me?
- What image does Jesus want to project to others about who he is?

For the disciples and for those looking ahead to the first day of school, what actually happens is much different from what's expected. The disciples certainly didn't expect Jesus to announce that one of them would betray him (Mark 14:18), nor did they expect him to predict that they will all falter in their faithfulness (14:27). What did the disciples think when Jesus broke the bread and said, "Take; this is my body," or when he took the cup and said, "This is my blood of the covenant" (Mark 14:22, 24)?

Surely this was a strange way to celebrate the Passover. Usually the Passover was an occasion to focus on freedom and deliverance and hope. The feast commemorated one of Israel's greatest triumphs. Jesus' disciples may have remembered this verse from Passovers past:

> Then the LORD said, "I have observed the misery of my people who are in Egypt; I have heard their cry on account of their taskmasters. Indeed, I know their sufferings, and I have come down to deliver them from the Egyptians."—Exodus 3:7-8*a*

All Jesus' talk about betrayal and denial and pouring out blood probably seemed out of place. What Jesus was saying to his disciples may have felt to them a lot like these words that students often hear on the first day of school:

- You will be required to . . .
- You will be expected to . . .
- Your entire grade will rest on . . .
- You will be asked to write a 10-page paper on . . .
- Each week, you will need to . . .

Amid the excitement surrounding the first day of school is the realization that the days ahead will not be easy. Students will have to work hard, make sacrifices, and set priorities. Along the way, they will face temptations and make mistakes; at times, they will probably feel overwhelmed. But students are also well aware of the rewards that come from perseverance and hard work: knowledge, skills, confidence, and opportunities to use these new-found gifts.

Followers of Jesus also are well aware of the rewards that come from being faithful and persevering, even when the Christian life seems overwhelming. Jesus gives us the opportunity to work alongside him, doing the work of God's kingdom, and spend eternity with him. While good teachers go to great lengths to help students get through the anxieties and challenges of the school year, Jesus does much more. Jesus gave his life to deliver us from slavery to sin and death; and Jesus continues to strengthen us and guide us. And whenever we celebrate Holy Communion, and eat from the bread and drink from the cup, we remember what Jesus has done and continues to do for us.

Biblical Foundation

On the first day of the [Festival of] Unleavened Bread, when the Passover lamb is sacrificed....While they were eating, [Jesus] took a loaf of bread, and after blessing it broke it, and gave it to them, and said, "Take; this is my body." Then he took a cup, and after giving thanks he gave it to them, and all of them all drank from it. He said to them, "This is my blood of the covenant, which is poured out for many. Truly I tell you, I will never drink of the fruit of the vine until that day when I drink it new in the kingdom of God."
—Mark 14:12a, 22-25

• *Video Presentation and Discussion (Optional)*
Watch the video segment "The Last Supper," from the *24 Hours That Changed the World* DVD. (Running Time: 11:25 minutes)

Sights
- The traditional site of the upper room (a vaulted room built by the crusaders in the twelfth century A.D.)
- A facsimile of a triclinium (u-shaped dining table common in the Roman world of the first century A.D.)
- A Seder plate

● *Key Insights*

Jesus specifically chose Peter and John to prepare the Passover meal.

It is thought that the site of the upper room where Jesus shared his last meal with his disciples is the same room where 120 disciples gathered on the Day of Pentecost to witness the coming of the Holy Spirit.

Although no one knows for certain, the room may have been the place where the disciples fled after Jesus was crucified.

The Last Supper was likely eaten around a triclinium. Reconstructing the seating of the group around a triclinium, we see that Jesus would have been flanked on his right by John and on his left by—Judas Iscariot.

According to Rabbi Amy Katz, the ritual Passover meal is intended to make the vital story of Israel's deliverance accessible to all those around the table.

- What did you learn about the Last Supper from this video?
- What thoughts and feelings do you experience when you take Holy Communion?
- How might a better knowledge and understanding of the Last Supper affect your experience of Holy Communion?
- What do you think about Judas Iscariot's being seated beside Jesus at the table, already determined to betray him?

Book Study and Discussion (Optional)

Prior to this session read the first chapter (pages 15–30) of *24 Hours That Changed the World,* by Adam Hamilton. Use the following questions to discuss this chapter with your group:

- What did you learn about the Last Supper?
- What did you learn about the relationship between the Jewish Passover Seder and the Christian sacrament of Holy Communion?

- On pages 26–30, Adam Hamilton describes the Eucharist, or Holy Communion, as a meal that defines who we are as Christians. How does our celebration of Holy Communion define who we are as Christians?
- How can you apply what you've learned in this chapter to your daily life?

Bringing the Scripture to My Life

- Passover remembers how God delivered the Israelites from slavery in Egypt. What "enslaves" you? (fear, doubt, temptation, and so forth)
- What does Jesus do with the bread and the wine? What does he teach or reveal to his disciples, using these items from the Passover meal?
- What is the relationship between the Passover feast and the Christian celebration of Holy Communion?
- Adam Hamilton, in *24 Hours That Changed the World,* writes, "I believe Jesus was expecting [Holy Communion] to define who we are." What does Holy Communion say about who Christians are and what Jesus has called us to do?

In transforming the Passover into the Eucharist, I believe Jesus was expecting this meal to define who we are. Through it, we remember that someone saved us; that our freedom came at the cost of a person; that God, walking in human flesh, suffered and died for us. This is the story we remember. It is a big story, and we have to get it if we are going to be a follower of Jesus Christ.

—Adam Hamilton, *24 Hours That Changed the World,* page 26

Going Deeper in Truth

Read Exodus 3:7.

- How do you think it makes God feel to see people suffering and in misery? How is God responding to our cries for help and for mercy?

Read John 15:12-17.

- Jesus calls his followers friends. How does thinking of yourself as Jesus' friend change your experience of Holy Communion?

Read Romans 5:1-8.

- Paul tells us here that Christ died for even the "ungodly." How does knowing that Christ's love is so large give us the strength to persevere through suffering (as Paul writes in verses 1-5)?

Experience Life in Community

Celebrate Holy Communion
Celebrate Holy Communion with your group during this session. Be sure to follow your denomination's procedures for this sacrament. (For example, if you are United Methodist, you will need an ordained elder to consecrate the Communion elements.) Invite a member of your pastoral staff to talk to your group about the importance and meaning of Holy Communion before breaking bread.

Celebrate a Love Feast
As an alternative to Holy Communion celebrate a love feast. A love feast is a Christian fellowship meal inspired by the meals that Jesus shared with his disciples and others throughout his earthly ministry.

To celebrate a love feast, gather around a common table. Set out baskets of bread, fruit, and other finger foods. Have a pitcher of water or juice or another beverage. Distribute the food and drink by passing around the baskets and the pitcher. When everyone has been served, have a time of prayer. Pray for the needs of your group, your community, and your world.

During the love feast, have volunteers read aloud Scriptures involving meals or banquets. Possibilities include:

Mark 6:30-44 (Jesus feeds the 5,000)
Luke 14:16-24 (the parable of the banquet)
John 6:25-35 ("I am the bread of life")

• *Making It Personal*

Here are two ways to put what you've learned into action in the coming week and beyond:

1. Choose a favorite snack that you really enjoy. The next time you have this snack, read Mark 14:22-25 as you do. Take time to reflect on the ways you are blessed and the things that you take for granted. You might even share this snack with someone else and reflect on the Scripture together. Hopefully, every time you eat this snack from now on, it will remind you of what Jesus has done for you.

2. Next time you go to a restaurant and the server comes to take your drink order, introduce yourself by your first name then ask the server if there is anything in his or her life that he or she would like you to be in prayer for. Tell the server that you will be saying a prayer before your meal and would be happy to pray for his or her concerns. Most people simply will reply with a polite "Thank you" or something like "Cool, I'll let you know." Some will name a prayer request, giving you an awesome opportunity to be in prayer for them. Others may not say anything. Regardless of how the server responds, he or she will get a good impression of what a Christian is and will know that someone cares enough to pray about them.

In pairs or groups of three, talk about other ways you can put what you've learned into action. How can you demonstrate Christ's love through food and fellowship? How can you be mindful of all the ways you are blessed and of all that Christ has done for you, even when you are anxious about what lies ahead?

Come up with two or three ideas. Then discuss these ideas with the other groups. Write in the space below one way that you will put what you have learned into action in the coming week and beyond.

• *Closing: Listening for God*

Close your eyes. Imagine that you are present at the Last Supper. Think about what Jesus' disciples are feeling. Think about a time in your own life when someone has done something unexpected for you. Think about how much you want to return the favor, how good it feels to be loved and to love in return. Live like that each day this week! Amen.

Session 2: The Garden of Gethsemane

✝

Getting Started

Goals for This Session

—Explore the meaning of Jesus' anguished prayer in the garden of Gethsemane.

—Understand that, though he was fully divine, Jesus was also fully human.

—Recognize our human weaknesses in the face of fear, doubt, and adversity. Accept that, with Christ's power, we can overcome anything we face.

Words to Know

Gethsemane: a garden on or near the Mount of Olives in Jerusalem where Jesus prayed before his trial and arrest

Cup: a burden that one must bear. (See Matthew 20:20-23.)

Introduction: The Garden of Gethsemane and the Night Before the Big Test

✝

You're sitting in class when you hear your teacher say, "Tomorrow is the day of the big test, and each of you should be ready. Come prepare to begin the test as soon as the bell sounds."

You hear these words; you know the test is tomorrow; you've even had the day marked on your calendar. But now that the test is upon you, you feel the anxiety building.

"I'm not ready, I'm not prepared. There must be some way out of this."

Jesus experienced these same feelings. But the test he faced was bigger than anything you or I could ever imagine. Our anxiety level climbs as the teacher reminds us what percentage of our grade the test accounts for. Concerned, we weigh our options:

- I've got all night. If I really focus, I'll be ready.
- I need to get Katie's notes. She takes incredible notes!
- Why didn't I spend more time preparing? Why did I wait until now?

And if we're being honest, for some of us, these thoughts also creep in:

- Maybe I could make some cheat sheets and slip them into my hand.

- Tomorrow is Friday. I could fake being sick and have the entire weekend to prepare.
- What if I let Katie know how desperate I am? Maybe she'll nudge her paper toward my desk so that I can sneak a peek at her answers.

Similar thoughts probably entered Christ's mind as he approached his ultimate test. Evil tempted Jesus in the wilderness and certainly would have tempted him during his final hours. Jesus asked his father that this "cup" be taken from him. ("Cup" here refers to a incredible burden.) But Jesus owns his mission and his commitment to his Father's will, and so he resists the temptation to take the easy way out. It's in this most vulnerable of moments that Jesus shows his power!

As imperfect people, we don't always face our tests and trials with the same courage and strength that Jesus showed in the garden of Gethsemane. Sometimes we give in to temptation, take the easy way out, or do things we know we shouldn't. Our weaknesses in these situations can make us feel inadequate and cause us to question whether Jesus still loves us. The good news is that Jesus does. Jesus, who was fully human as well as fully divine, understands our weakness and knows what it's like to be tempted. And Jesus is patient with us, much as he was patient with Thomas.

Thomas is best known for doubting Jesus' resurrection (John 20:24-29). But earlier in John's Gospel, Thomas is eager to follow Jesus, even if it means dying with him (11:16). Thomas isn't weak or unfaithful. He's just human. And Jesus understands this.

> But Thomas (who was called the Twin), one of the twelve, was not with them when Jesus came. So the other disciples told him, "We have seen the Lord." But he said to them, "Unless I see the mark of the nails in his hands, and put my finger in the mark of the nails and my hand in his side, I will not believe."

A week later his disciples were again in the house, and Thomas was with them. Although the doors were shut, Jesus came and stood among them and said, "Peace be with you." Then he said to Thomas, "Put your finger here and see my hands. Reach out your hand and put it in my side. Do not doubt but believe." Thomas answered him, "My Lord and my God!" Jesus said to him, "Have you believed because you have seen me? Blessed are those who have not seen and yet have come to believe."

Upon learning that Thomas was unwilling to believe the news of the Resurrection without seeing "the mark of the nail in [Jesus'] hands" and putting his finger "in the mark of the nails," Jesus could have said, "OK, Thomas. That's your choice." Instead he meets Thomas where he is—mired in doubt and disbelief. Jesus goes even further, actually allowing Thomas to touch his wounds. Overcome by Jesus' love, Thomas cries out, "My Lord and my God!"

It's easy to doubt God's love when we sin and make mistakes. But God loves us enough to meet us where we are, hoping that we will open ourselves to God's redeeming love.

Biblical Foundation

Then Jesus went with them to a place called Gethsemane; and he said to his disciples, "Sit here while I go over there and pray" He took with him Peter and the two sons of Zebedee, and began to be grieved and agitated. Then he said to them, "I am deeply grieved, even to death; remain here, and stay awake with me." And going a little farther, he threw himself on the ground and prayed, "My Father, if it is possible, let this cup pass from me; yet not what I want but what you want." Then he came to the disciples and found them sleeping; and he said to Peter, "So, could you not stay awake with me one hour? Stay awake and pray that you may not come into the time of trial; the spirit indeed is willing, but the flesh is weak." Again he went away for the second time and prayed, "My Father, if this cannot pass unless I drink it, your will be done." Again he came and found them sleeping, for their eyes were heavy. So leaving them again, he went away and prayed for the third time, saying the same words. Then he came to the disciples and said to them, "Are you still sleeping and taking your rest? See, the hour is at hand, and the Son of Man is betrayed into the hands of sinners. Get up, let us be going. See, my betrayer is at hand."—Matthew 26:36-46

Video Presentation and Discussion (Optional)

Watch the video segment "The Garden of Gethsemane," from the *24 Hours That Changed the World* DVD. (Running Time: 6:57 minutes)

Sights

- The garden of Gethsemane
- A 3000-year-old olive tree in Gethsemane
- The Church of All Nations, particularly the stars painted on the ceiling in the Church of All Nations
- The rock considered the traditional site of Jesus' prayer in Gethsemane

Key Insights

Approaching the Holy Land as a pilgrim allows you to place yourself in the story, to imagine yourself trying to stay awake under an olive tree, or to kneel at the very place Christ may have thrown himself on the ground in agony.

Jesus began his public ministry by being tempted by the devil. Here in the garden, Jesus was tempted once again: "You don't have to suffer. You don't have to die. Just run!"

25

The Church of All Nations was designated to take pilgrims back to that night in the garden. The interior is dark. The ceiling is full of stars. Below a large mosaic of Christ kneeling in prayer is a large rock that pilgrims can kneel before and touch.

In both the garden of Eden and the garden of Gethsemane, the crucial question was, "God's will or not?"

- How does this video give you a better sense of the temptation that Jesus faced in the garden of Gethsemane?
- When do you have trouble staying awake and alert?
- How can we stay awake and alert so that we're ready when Jesus calls us to do something?

Book Study and Discussion (Optional)

Prior to this session, read the second chapter (pages 31–44) of *24 Hours That Changed the World,* by Adam Hamilton. Use the following questions to discuss this chapter with your group:

- What did you learn from this chapter about Jesus' prayer in the garden of Gethsemane?
- What did you learn about who Jesus is and what he might have been feeling?
- How does knowing that Jesus suffered anguish and temptation and that he can relate to us when we are hurting bring you comfort?
- How can you apply to your life what you've learned in this chapter?

Bringing the Scripture to My Life

- Jesus prays in agony. He's about to face the biggest test ever, and he even asks his Father to take this "cup" from him so that he won't have to go through with it. Why are times of stress and vulnerability times when we are most likely to be tempted?

- What situations that you face distress you or agitate you? Are you weaker or stronger in these situations? Why?

- What temptations do you face during challenging and stressful times? How do you find the strength to face these temptations?

- What, do you think, does Jesus mean when he says, "The spirit is willing, but the flesh is weak"?

- How do you find the strength to face tests, challenges, and obstacles?

- How does Jesus give you comfort and help you recover when you mess up or give in to temptation?

- Can we allow Jesus to be a person? The church always asserted that, in Jesus, God had become "fully human." What does it mean for Jesus to be fully human?

- How would you feel if you knew that within a few hours you would be tortured; publicly humiliated; and then subjected to one of the cruelest, least humane, and most painful forms of capital punishment ever devised by human beings?

- What if you knew that your death would leave open the possibility that terrible atrocities would be committed that you might have prevented? Can you sense the anguish Jesus must have felt?

The idea that Jesus was in anguish, pleading with God, is unsettling to many Christians. For some, the scene evokes great compassion. For others, the image of Jesus asking God to take the cup of suffering from him and his apparent anxiety over the Crucifixion seems to lack nobility and courage. For still others, the image may even appear to indicate a lack of faith. They would perhaps expect Jesus to face his torture and death without agitation or fear.

—Adam Hamilton, *24 Hours That Changed the World,* page 37

Going Deeper in Truth

Read Job 19:25-27.

• Job has been through almost unimaginable suffering. (See Job 1:6-22.) How does he stay focused on God?

Read 1 Corinthians 10:13.

• Paul reminds the Church body at Corinth here "God is faithful" and "will not let [them] be tested beyond [their] strength." How has God given you comfort and relief during times of doubt or disbelief?

Read 1 Peter 2:21.

• Peter tells us to follow Christ's example. How can we do this? What changes might you need to make to follow Christ's example?

Experience Life in Community

Have a Pow-Wow

Traditionally, a *pow-wow* is a gathering to celebrate the culture of America's native peoples. This is something different.

Gather into a circle, and invite each person to talk about his or her "pows" and "wows." Pows are anything that involves loss, pain, hurt, or stress. Wows are gifts, blessings, and joys.

Have someone write down everyone's pows and wows and send out the list to everyone in the group. In the coming week, pray for one another, give thanks for the wows, and ask for the strength to endure the pows.

Making It Personal

This week try a "reverse fast." Fasting is a spiritual practice in which a person does without something (often food) as a way to worship and focus on God. Doing without something we normally take for granted reminds us that all of the good things we have are gifts and blessings from God. A reverse fast is also an act of worship and devotion, but it involves taking something on instead of giving something up. Here are some suggestions of things you can take on this week:

1. Stop and spend time alone with God (TAG) each day this week, even if just for five minutes each day. During your TAG, be sure to listen more than you speak.
2. Read a chapter of Scripture each day. If you're new to the Bible, start with the Gospel of Mark. (Mark is the shortest Gospel and was probably the first Gospel written. It's a great way to become familiar with Jesus' life, ministry, and teachings.)
3. Each day at lunch, offer to take up someone's tray or to take care of his or her trash and recyclables.
4. Write a note to a teacher or to your principal to thank that person for what he or she does.
5. Learn about a crisis facing your community or another part of the country or world. Each day, check the news for stories about this crisis and spend time in prayer for all of the people affected.

Closing: Listening for God

John Wesley, a great faith leader in the 1700s, prayed the following prayer. He called it his covenant prayer. *Covenant* means "a binding agreement between two parties." Jesus invites us to be in a covenant relationship with him.

Pray this prayer to close your time together, and pray it each day throughout the coming week:

I am no longer my own, but thine.

Put me to what thou wilt; rank me with whom thou wilt.

Put me to doing; put me to suffering.

Let me be employed for thee or laid aside for thee,

exalted for thee or brought low for thee.

Let me be full; let me be empty.

Let me have all things; let me have nothing.

I freely and heartily yield all things to thy pleasure and disposal.

And now, O glorious and blessed God, Father, Son, and Holy Spirit,

thou art mine; and I am thine.

So be it.

And the covenant which I have made on earth,

let it be ratified in heaven.

Amen.

Session 3: Condemned by the Righteous

✝

Getting Started

Goals for This Session

—Explore Mark's account of Jesus' trial before the high priest Caiaphas and the Sanhedrin, especially in the context of bullying, gossip, and judgment.

—Understand why and how the religious powers in Jerusalem exercised their need for power and control and how they condemned an innocent man.

—Recognize how fear and a need to be accepted tempt us to remain silent in the face of wrongdoing and to deny the truth of Christ.

Words to Know

Sanhedrin: a council of leaders. The Sanhedrin in Jerusalem was a group of religious and/or political leaders. Mark's Gospel specifically mentions chief priests, elders, and scribes (14:53).

Introduction:
Jesus' Trial and Injustice

✝

Yes! Lunch time! You head to the cafeteria, excited to see your friends, get your favorite soda, talk about Friday night's football game or the new movie you want to see, and take a deep breath after the big test you just powered through.

That's when you see it: a kid being picked on, someone uttering a racial slur, or a practical joke in some stage of development. Even if the practical joke seems fun and creative, you know that its victim will be hurt and embarrassed.

Each day, these situations test our resolve. It is as though we are on trial: The classroom or cafeteria becomes a courtroom, where our peers, our teachers, or ever our own hearts will render judgment.

Too often in these trials we are found guilty—guilty of standing aside quietly while others are picked on, belittled, or pushed away. Maybe we say to ourselves:

- "Thank God that's not me."
- "He gets picked on all the time. He's used to it. No big deal."
- "If I pretend that I didn't see or hear anything, I can slip by and not get involved."

Evil and injustice bank on people standing by and doing nothing, whether out of fear or convenience. It's amazing what our conscience can accept when we don't have to look directly at the prank or the abuse.

But Jesus calls us to live differently, to confront injustice and stand up for the things Jesus cares about. When Jesus was on trial before the high priest Caiaphas, he knew what was coming. He faced his trial boldly and courageously, even as those he trusted most abandoned and denied him.

True story: A young woman named Sally often went to the movies with her mom on Friday nights. Sally usually looked forward to these movie nights, but had no idea that one Friday night at the movies would transform her life and make her into a change agent for God.

That Friday, Sally and her mother saw the movie *Amazing Grace*, which tells the true story of 18th-century abolitionist William Wilberforce. An abolitionist is one who fights to abolish slavery. And Wilberforce's long fight to end the slave trade in the United Kingdom ultimately played a big role in eliminating slavery on both sides of the Atlantic.

Amazing Grace recounts Wilberforce's struggles with his call to serve God in ministry and his desire to serve his people as a representative in British parliament. His faith compels him to fight the slave trade, but he knows that doing so will make him unpopular in Parliament. But, in a powerful scene, a group of ministers and abolitionists visit with Wilberforce and show him that, being a member of Parliament, he is in a unique position to take a stand for the cause of abolition. Wilberforce spends much of the rest of his life fighting slavery, often calling on one of his friends and mentors, John Newton, for advice and support. (John Newton, the author of the popular hymn "Amazing Grace," had been involved in the slave trade until his faith persuaded him to become an Anglican priest and join the abolition movement.) Wilberforce ultimately succeeds in the work God has called him to do. After two decades, Parliament passes the Slave Trade Act, which has a global impact.

Sally left the movie with an overwhelming need to get involved in the current-day abolition movement. She researched where and how slavery exists today. Her passion and God's call led her to join the fight against teen sex trafficking, a form of slavery in which young people are kidnapped and forced into prostitution. Sex trafficking takes place even in countries where such practices have long been illegal, including the United States.

Sally now gathers a group at her school devoted to abolition. The group calls itself "Clapham Sect: Phase 2." The group considers itself a continuation of the original "Clapham Sect," which was William Wilberforce's group of 18th- and 19th-century Anglican abolitionists. (You can find more information on Sally's group and how you can get involved at *www.csp2.net.*)

Sally's passion to care for those who are being abused, exploited, bullied, pushed down, and forgotten has taken her as far as India, where she traveled as part of her college studies. Sex trafficking is prevalent in India. Sally desires to learn as much as possible about this injustice so that she can more effectively fight it.

Sally's story is just one example of how we can stand up against evil— evil that is banking on us to walk by.

Jesus faced trial, shame, and suffering on behalf of each one of us. Yet, when Jesus was on trial in front of the high priest and the Sanhedrin (a council of Jerusalem religious leaders), his closest followers were afraid to take a stand on his behalf. Peter, whom Jesus had called "the rock" and who was present with Jesus at his transfiguration, actually denied Jesus three times (Mark 14:66-72) while Jesus was on trial.

Jesus stood up for a world that wouldn't stand up for him. And he continued to love the disciples who abandoned him, and even Peter who denied him. This extraordinary love, grace, and forgiveness would give Jesus' disciples the courage to put their lives and reputations on the line to spread the good news of Christ and to preach and heal in Jesus' name.

Biblical Foundation

They took Jesus to the high priest; and all the chief priests, the elders, and the scribes were assembled.... Now the chief priests and the whole council were looking for testimony against Jesus to put him to death; but they found none.... But he was silent and did not answer. Again the high priest asked him, "Are you the Messiah, the Son of the Blessed One?" Jesus said, "I am; and

> 'you will see the Son of Man
> seated at the right hand of the Power,'
> and 'coming with the clouds of heaven.'"

Then the high priest tore his clothes and said, "Why do we still need witnesses? You have heard his blasphemy! What is your decision?" All of them condemned him as deserving death. Some began to spit on him, to blindfold him, and to strike him, saying to him, "Prophesy!" The guards also took him over and beat him.

While Peter was below in the courtyard, one of the servant-girls of the high priest came by. When she saw Peter warming himself, she stared at him and said, "You also were with Jesus, the man from Nazareth." But he denied it, saying, "I do not know or understand what you are talking about." And he went out into the forecourt. Then the cock crowed.... But again he denied it. Then after a little while the bystanders again said to Peter, "Certainly you are one of them; for you are a Galilean." But he began to curse, and he swore an oath, "I do not know this man you are talking about." At that moment the cock crowed for the second time. Then Peter remembered that Jesus had said to him, "Before the cock crows twice, you will deny me three times." And he broke down and wept.—Mark 14:53, 55, 61-68, 70-72

Video Presentation and Discussion (Optional)

Watch the video segment "Condemned by the Righteous," from the *24 Hours That Changed the World* DVD. (Running Time: 9:15 minutes)

Sights

- The steep stone incline leading up to Caiaphas' house
- Outside the ruins of the site believed to be the palace home of the high priest Caiaphas
- The pit discovered beneath the ruins of Caiaphas' house, likely a holding place for prisoners awaiting trial
- Inside the Church of Peter at Gallicantu
- The statue of Peter, which depicts his three denials

Key Insights

The walk from the garden of Gethsemane, across the Kidron Valley, and up to the high priest's home takes about twenty minutes; Jesus would have walked at night, probably barefoot.

In antiquity, a prison was often no more than a pit or dry cistern. Jesus was likely lowered into a pit like the one found beneath the ruins of Caiaphas' house and perhaps held for five, six, or seven hours.

While we focus on Peter denying Christ during his appearance before the Sanhedrin, we should remember that Peter was the only disciple to come to the place where Jesus was to be tried.

- How does this video give you a better idea of what Jesus went through before and during his trial?
- Imagine what it would have been like to walk barefoot for twenty minutes then to be lowered into a pit, hands shackled above your head, for several hours. What, do you think, might Jesus have thought and felt? What would you think and feel had you been in that situation?

- Think about the statue of Peter that you saw in the video. How did the sculptor show Peter's denials?

- The video includes the statement, "If there is hope for Peter, there is hope for us." When have you felt like Peter, as though you turned your back on your faith or on a close friend or family member? How does what you know about Jesus give you comfort?

- How can you prepare yourself so that you can stand firm in your faith, even when it would be easier to walk away (or to deny your faith)?

Book Study and Discussion (Optional)

Prior to this session, read the third chapter (pages 45–59) of *24 Hours That Changed the World,* by Adam Hamilton. Use the following questions to discuss this chapter with your group:

- What did you learn from this chapter about Jesus' trial that you didn't know before?

- How was Jesus a threat to the people in power in Jerusalem?

- How is Jesus still a threat to people today?

- When Caiaphas asks Jesus, "Are you the Messiah, the Son of the Blessed One?" Jesus answers, "I am" (Mark 14:61-62). These two words are very powerful and would have reminded the council of God's answer to Moses when Moses asked about God's name, "I am who I am" (Exodus 3:14). Throughout John's Gospel, Jesus makes "I am" statements (such as "I am the bread that came down from heaven" [6:41] and "I am the resurrection and the life" [11:25]). Imagine Jesus speaking directly to you. How might he complete the sentence, "I am _____"?

- What did you learn from this chapter about Peter's denial of Jesus?

- How can you apply what you learned from this chapter to your day-to-day life?

Bringing the Scripture to My Life

- In Mark 14, Jesus is condemned to die. He is beaten, and he is deserted by his closest friends. One of his closest and most trusted disciples denies him. What are ways that you have deserted or denied Christ in your life?

- As you walk the halls of your school, seeing others put down or picked on, how will you respond? How will you resist the temptation to walk away or ignore what's going on? How can you be part of stopping this injustice?

- Reread Sally's story (pages 33–34). Sally was passionate about ending slavery, and especially sex trafficking. What injustices are you most passionate about? (Examples might include hunger, poverty, and people dying of treatable illnesses.) How might God be calling you or preparing you to do something about these injustices?

In the Gospels of Matthew, Mark, and Luke, we find that as Jesus was led away, the disciples fled—except for Peter. Peter followed the guards as they took Jesus to Caiaphas' house. He clung to the shadows; but when he got there, he steeled himself and entered the high priest's very courtyard to see what was happening. Do you see the courage it took to do that? Would you have walked into the courtyard knowing you could be put to death for being a disciple of Jesus?

Still, Peter's courage lasted only up to a point. Warming himself at the fire, he stood among the Temple guards as the trial went on; but he was probably doing his best to conceal his identity. Then, when a servant girl called attention to him, he began to waver. "You also were with that Nazarene, Jesus," she said. "I know you were" (Mark 14:67, TNIV). At that moment, fear took over. Knowing that he was in danger of being harmed, Peter would not stand up as one of Jesus' disciples.

—Adam Hamilton, *24 Hours That Changed the World*, page 57

Going Deeper in Truth

Read Ephesians 4:17-24.

- In this letter to the church in Ephesus, Paul tells his readers to put away their old life and to "clothe" themselves with a new life. What old attitudes and behaviors do you need to put away?
- What does it mean to live a life of "true righteousness and holiness"? What does it mean to be righteous and holy when we come face-to-face with evil and injustice?

Read Matthew 25:31-46.

- Jesus teaches us that, whatever we do for the "least of these" (the hungry and sick and imprisoned), we also do for him. How does this Scripture change the way you think about people you see every day? How will this Scripture change the way you act toward these people?

Read John 21:5-17.

- Peter had three times denied knowing Jesus. Here Jesus asks Peter three times (one for each denial), "Do you love me?" Imagine for a moment that Jesus is asking you, "Do you love me?" once for each time you have denied him? How would you answer? How would you show your love for Jesus through your actions?

Experience Life in Community

Confession Circle

Take time to reflect on the many ways we may have denied Christ just as Peter did. Here are some possibilities:

- A time when someone has asked, "Are you a Christian?" and we have dodged the question.

- A time when we have passed up an opportunity to tell people about something going on at our church.
- A time when we have been embarrassed or reluctant to talk about our church life.
- A time when we saw someone being bullied, and we walked by without doing anything.
- A time when we have skipped worship or daily prayers or a Bible study because we wanted to do something else.
- A time when we failed to speak up for someone being picked on.

Gather into a circle. Go around the circle, having each person name one way in which he or she has denied Christ. No one should name names or say anything that would embarrass a classmate or peer. Following each of these confessions, the group should respond, "In Christ's name, you are forgiven."

Then invite one person to say a prayer thanking Christ for his courage and his willingness to sacrifice everything on our behalf, thanking Christ for being present with us in the person of the Holy Spirit during times of trial, and asking Christ for the strength to be holy and righteous when we see evil and injustice.

Closing: Taking Action for God

Choose someone who has been picked on at your school. Lift up his or her name in prayer each day, listening for how God is calling you to act. It may be that God is calling you to become this person's friend, or at the very least to stand up for this person when he or she is being picked on, talked about, or belittled. How might you be an answer to prayer for this person?

Session 4: Jesus, Barabbas, and Pilate

✝

Getting Started

Goals for This Session

—Explore the Gospel accounts of Jesus' trial before the Roman governor Pontius Pilate.

—Understand Jesus' determination to suffer and face death at the hands of the religious and political authorities in Jerusalem.

—Recognize the purpose of Jesus' suffering: redemption for all.

Words to Know

Antonia Fortress: a tower fortress near the Temple in Jerusalem that was renovated by King Herod the Great and named for Roman general Mark Antony (who had appointed Herod king of Judea)

Suffering servant: a servant described in three separate passages by the prophet Isaiah (42:1-9; 50:4-11; 52:13–53:12), whom Christians traditionally identify as Jesus Christ.

Introduction: Jesus' Trial Before Pilate and Your Daily Life

†

How many children have said to their parents, "I want to be treated like an adult," only to be told in return, "If you want to be treated like an adult, act like an adult"?

From the Author

During my ninth-grade year, my grades slipped. My parents' response was to institute a weekly progress report. Each Friday, I had to carry a worksheet around to every class and have each of my teachers write a note about my academic progress in that class. These notes from teachers, along with my ability to turn in my homework on time and get good grades on tests, would determine whether I would be free for the weekend. Regardless of any plans I had made for Friday or Saturday evening, I'd be stuck at home if I didn't keep up my grades and behave in class. One bad report from one teacher meant a lonely and boring weekend at home.

I wanted freedom. I wanted to be my own person. But freedom and independence require responsibility.

Often we have to do things that are difficult or unpleasant for the sake of freedom. When he stood trial before Pilate, Jesus knew that he would be condemned to die. He knew that he would face suffering and humiliation. But Jesus didn't try to get out of it. He said very little in his trial at the Antonia Fortress and said nothing in his defense. He understood his mission and his responsibility and would not be deterred. For Jesus, accepting responsibility meant standing alone before a crowd that was demanding that he be executed—a crowd that yelled for Pilate to release the murderous insurrectionist Barabbas instead of Jesus, who was innocent.

Sometimes taking responsibility means standing alone for what we know to be true. In a court of law in the United States, we pledge to "tell the truth, the whole truth, and nothing but the truth." This three-part legal statement of truth helps us, as followers of Christ, better understand what it means to be truthful. First, as Christians, we must tell the truth; it's great to know and understand what is true, but we must also speak. Second, the entire truth is critical—not just the parts that are comfortable or convenient. Third, we shouldn't let our opinions and biases get in the way of the truth.

The truth that Jesus stood for was God's love for humankind. He spoke this truth throughout his life and ministry. And Jesus stood for the whole truth, including the part that said he must suffer and die for the forgiveness of sins. Along the way, Jesus resisted the temptation to stray from the truth or to take the easy way out.

Standing up for the truth of Christ—the truth, the whole truth, and nothing but the truth—can make us unpopular. Jesus stood alone amid a crowd screaming for him to be crucified, and he never wavered from the truth.

Biblical Foundation

As soon as it was morning, the chief priests held a consultation with the elders and scribes and the whole council. They bound Jesus, led him away, and handed him over to Pilate. Pilate asked him, "Are you the King of the Jews?" He answered him, "You say so." Then the chief priests accused him of many things. Pilate asked him again, "Have you no answer? See how many charges they bring against you." But Jesus made no further reply, so that Pilate was amazed.

Now at the festival he used to release a prisoner for them, anyone for whom they asked. Now a man called Barabbas was in prison with the rebels who had committed murder during the insurrection. So the crowd came and began to ask Pilate to do for them according to his custom. Then he answered them, "Do you want me to release for you the King of the Jews?" For he realized that it was out of jealousy that the chief priests had handed him over. But the chief priests stirred up the crowd to have him release Barabbas for them instead. Pilate spoke to them again, "Then what do you wish me to do with the man you call the King of the Jews?" They shouted back, "Crucify him!" Pilate asked them, "Why, what evil has he done?" But they shouted all the more, "Crucify him!" So Pilate, wishing to satisfy the crowd, released Barabbas for them; and after flogging Jesus, he handed him over to be crucified.—Mark 15:1-15

Video Presentation and Discussion (Optional)

Watch the video segment "Jesus, Barabbas, and Pilate," from the *24 Hours That Changed the World* DVD. (Running Time: 9:10 minutes)

Sights

- The opening shot of a busy street—a sharp contrast to the likely empty street Jesus walked, early in the morning, from the house of Caiaphas to the Fortress Antonia, the traditional site of his trial before Pilate
- A scale model of the city of Jerusalem and the Temple as they looked in Jesus' day

- A priest leading pilgrims along the Via Dolorosa (which is Latin for "Way of Suffering")
- The stone pavement (called *lithostrotos*) where the crowd gathered for the trial before Pilate

Key Insights

The Via Dolorosa, or the Way of Suffering, marks the steps of Jesus from his condemnation before Pilate to his burial.

The Stations of the Cross, developed by the Franciscans in the fourteenth century, is a devotional journey of fourteen stops, allowing pilgrims to retrace Jesus' journey along the Way of Suffering.

Pilate gave the crowd a choice between Jesus Barabbas and his call to take up arms and Jesus of Nazareth and his call to love. The crowd chose violence.

Imagine the sound echoing off the stone pavement, "Crucify him!"

- How does this video give you a better idea of what Jesus went through during his trial before Pilate?
- Had you been in the crowd that morning, how, do you think, would you have responded? Would you have taken a stand for Jesus, or would you have joined the crowd in calling for Pilate to release Barabbas?
- Why, do you think, did early Christians develop devotional exercises such as the Stations of the Cross? Does our congregation do Stations of the Cross during Holy Week?
- How can you get a better sense of what Jesus experienced and suffered by retracing his steps (either by watching this video, by going through the stations of the cross, or by remembering Jesus journey to the cross in some other way)?

Book Study and Discussion (Optional)

Prior to this session, read the fourth chapter (pages 61–78) of *24 Hours That Changed the World*, by Adam Hamilton. Use the following questions to discuss this chapter with your group:

- What did you learn from this chapter about Jesus' trial before Pilate that you didn't know before?
- Why, do you think, did Jesus say so little in his own defense?
- How does the sketch of the Suffering Servant in Isaiah describe the suffering and death of Jesus?

Bringing the Scripture to My Life

- Jesus is on trial, and the people are against him. When have you had an experience where choosing the right and responsible path was unpopular?
- What, do you think, was Jesus thinking and feeling as the crowd turned against him?
- What can we learn from Jesus' example about standing up for what is true and right even when doing so is unpopular?
- Where can you find strength and courage when you feel as though the world is against you?

We are meant to look at the cross and see both God's great love and the costliness of grace and to find our hearts changed by what God has done for us. We are meant, as a result of understanding that cost, to serve God with humble gratitude, and to long, as we see Jesus suffer, never to sin again. And yet, of course, we will sin again and call again upon the grace of God revealed on the cross. Like Barabbas, we walk away free because of the suffering of an innocent man.

—Adam Hamilton, *24 Hours That Changed the World*, page 68

Going Deeper in Truth

Read Matthew 27:24-26.

- What do you think of Pilate's response to the crowd's demands to crucify Jesus and release Barabbas? Is Pilate truly innocent of Jesus' blood?
- When have you tried to pass the blame for something for which you were at least partially responsible?

Read Ephesians 4:1-16.

- When are you tempted to go down the wrong path?
- How can you avoid being "tossed to and fro" by "trickery" and "deceitful scheming"? What can you do to stay connected to Christ?

Experience Life in Community

Burn Sins

Have on hand a candle, a lighter, pens or pencils, and one piece of flash paper for each person to participate in a sin burning. (Flash paper is paper that burns instantly without leaving behind ash. You can buy it at most magic or novelty shops or through many online retailers.)

Have each person write on a small piece of flash paper several sins and mistakes for which he or she is guilty.

Light the candle. Ask each participant to come forward, one at a time, one at a time, to bring his or her sins (the ones written on the flash paper) to the flame. As the rest of the participants say in unison, "In the name of Jesus Christ, you are forgiven," the participant should hold the flash paper to the flame and watch his or her sins disappear.

After everyone has burned his or her sins, a volunteer should read aloud 1 John 1:9: "If we confess our sins, he who is faithful and just will forgive us our sins and cleanse us from all unrighteousness."

Making It Personal

This week, identify one person in your family whom you have wronged. Maybe you said something hurtful, didn't do a chore you were supposed to do, or told a lie. Have the courage to ask this person for forgiveness. Repent of this wrongdoing by confessing and making a commitment to live differently in the future.

Closing: Listening for God

Close with a "popcorn prayer." Open with a word of thanks to God for what God has done through Christ and for Jesus' courage, determination , and devotion to the truth while he was on trial. Then invite each person to name something for which he or she is thankful (in a word or phrase) related to this session.

Session 5: The Torture and Humiliation of the King

✝

Getting Started

Goals for This Session

—Explore the Gospel accounts of Jesus' humiliation at the hands of Roman soldiers on his way to the cross.

—Understand the role of Jesus' suffering in the redemption of the world.

—Recognize how our choices can bring pain to others and discuss how we can guard against them.

Words to Know

Atonement: the way in which Christ, through his suffering, death, and resurrection, reconciles sinners to God

Golgotha: an Aramaic word meaning "the skull" that was used to describe the site where Jesus was crucified. Golgotha was near Jerusalem but outside of the city walls.

Introduction: Jesus' Humiliation and Sarcasm

✝

Have you ever said something just to push someone's buttons or to hurt someone deliberately? Have you ever said something to get a laugh at someone else's expense, only to realize afterward how deeply it hurt him or her?

Most everyone—including pastors and parents and teachers—has been guilty of embarrassing or humiliating someone. We know that this sort of behavior is wrong; but we do it anyway, thinking that it will boost our self-esteem or earn us the favor or our peers.

What were the Roman soldiers feeling as they were terrorizing Jesus? Did it give them some sort of sick and twisted satisfaction?

It's easy for us to look down on these soldiers and judge them. But we all have been guilty of similar actions, even if what we have done wasn't nearly as cruel as what the soldiers did. Sometimes our culture even celebrates belittling and humiliating others. One particular type of mocking and cruelty that our culture promotes is sarcasm.

Dictionary.com defines *sarcasm* as "harsh or bitter derision or irony" and as "a sharply ironical taunt; sneering or cutting remark." By definition, sarcasm is meant to be harsh, to taunt, and to offend.

Most of us, while walking through the halls at school, have thought of funny, sarcastic things to say to passing friends and peers. Some of these remarks we make in jest; others are intended to hurt or embarrass. Sometimes remarks that we don't intend to be hurtful still inflict damage. A snarky comment about the football player who dropped a key pass in the big game or the girl who seems to have a different boyfriend every week or the kid who's obsessed with studying and keeping her grades up can be as painful as the lashings that the Roman soldiers gave Jesus.

It's easy to give into the temptation to ridicule, belittle, and humiliate others. Insults and pranks get big laughs on television and in movies. And we often get the false impression that having fun at someone else's expense will make us feel better about ourselves or will impress others.

From the Author

Recently in the ministry I serve, a young lady took a stand. At first, her peers belittled her for doing it. But in the end, they praised her for her strength.

Laurie was on the cheerleading squad at her school. When the new uniforms came in, the coach handed them out and sent the squad into the dressing room to try them on. All of the girls on the squad, except Laurie, seemed excited to have their new uniforms. She was embarrassed. She had never worn anything so revealing and wondered why the coach had chosen such skimpy uniforms.

Laurie decided to take a stand, knowing that she may be alone in doing so. She came out of the locker room wearing a t-shirt, with leggings on underneath. None of the other girls had done this and most of them looked at her strangely.

Laurie told her coach that she could not wear this uniform as it was against her Christian convictions concerning appropriate dress. The coach told Laurie that, if she did not wear the uniform as it was meant to be worn, she couldn't be on the squad.

Laurie went home and told her mother what had happened. Her mother supported her decision, and they both talked to the other girls and their parents. Laurie and her mother discovered that the other girls were embarrassed as well.

At the next practice, many of the girls showed up with t-shirts and leggings on underneath. This forced the coach to change the uniforms. Laurie found the strength from within to stand up for what was right, and good, and true. She didn't take the easy way out or give in to the temptation to conform, even when threatened with losing her spot on the cheerleading squad.

When we call upon the strength of the Holy Spirit we have the power to not give in to actions that hurt God and others. Jesus', in his suffering, torture, and humiliation, showed great fortitude and set for us an example to follow.

Biblical Foundation

Then the soldiers led him into the courtyard of the palace (that is, the governor's headquarters); and they called together the whole cohort. And they clothed him in a purple cloak; and after twisting some thorns into a crown, they put it on him. And they began saluting him, "Hail, King of the Jews!" They struck his head with a reed, spat upon him, and knelt down in homage to him. After mocking him, they stripped him of the purple cloak and put his own clothes on him. Then they led him out to crucify him.

They compelled a passer-by, who was coming in from the country, to carry his cross; it was Simon of Cyrene, the father of Alexander and Rufus. Then they brought Jesus to the place called Golgotha (which means the place of a skull). And they offered him wine mixed with myrrh; but he did not take it.—Mark 15:16-23

Video Presentation and Discussion (Optional)

Watch the video segment "The Torture and Humiliation of the King," from the *24 Hours That Changed the World* DVD. (Running Time: 9:06 minutes)

Sights

- A whip and whipping post similar to those used by the Romans in the first century A.D.
- The Chapel of Flagellation and its three stained-glass windows depicting Pontius Pilate; Barabbas; and Jesus bound to a Roman column, with a crown of thorns on the ceiling
- The pieces of a Roman cross: the vertical beam (*stipes*) and the horizontal beam (*patibulum*)
- Gordon's Calvary, a skull-shaped rock formation near an unfinished tomb, which was proposed in the late 1800s as the site where Christ was crucified

Key Insights

The Gospels say very little about the flogging of Jesus, and their accounts are slightly different.

We see in the beating and humiliation of Jesus evidence of an evil kind of cruelty in which human beings torment one whose very existence is a challenge to them.

The horizontal beam of the cross Jesus carried weighed nearly 100 pounds. It is likely that, after Jesus attempted to carry it some distance, Simon of Cyrene was pressed into service.

John tells us that Jesus carried his own cross, undoubtedly wanting readers to see the connection to Isaac carrying the wood on which he was about to be sacrificed.

- How does this video give you a better idea of what Jesus went through as he was tortured and humiliated on his way to the cross?
- How do you imagine the scene in which Jesus was mocked? How do you imagine Jesus responded to this cruelty?
- What does the example of Simon of Cyrene teach us about Christian discipleship?

Book Study and Discussion (Optional)

Prior to this session, read the fifth chapter (pages 79–94) of *24 Hours That Changed the World,* by Adam Hamilton. Use the following questions to discuss this chapter with your group:

- What did you learn from this chapter about the torture and humiliation Jesus faced prior to his crucifixion?
- What, do you think, was worse: the physical torture Jesus suffered through or the emotional torture? Why?
- What are some current-day examples of torture and humiliation? How can people bring themselves to do such horrible things to other human beings?
- What can we learn from the example of Simon of Cyrene?
- What does this chapter teach us about sacrificial love and about what Jesus did on our behalf?

Bringing the Scripture to My Life

- Jesus is not only flogged (beaten) but mocked as "the King of the Jews." What are some ways in which we mock Jesus? How do we mock Jesus through the way we treat others or fail to follow Jesus' commandments?
- When are you, like the Roman soldiers, guilty of mocking or taunting others?

- For what reasons do people embarrass and humiliate one another?

- How can you set a positive example of how to treat other people, particularly those whom you're tempted to mock or humiliate?

- What can we learn from how Jesus responds to torture and taunting? How should you respond when people mock you or try to embarrass you? How can you stand up for yourself without resorting to revenge or violence?

The brokenness of humanity is not the only word we are meant to hear in this story. . . . We are also meant to see the love of the One who suffers for us, as well as his determination to save us from ourselves and from our sin. Jesus' suffering and death were not accidental. He chose the path he knew would end in his Passion. He faced the flagrum, the crown, and the cross with determination, silence, and dignity. He stood naked as if to say, "Do you see the extent of the Father's love yet? Do you understand that I have come so that you might finally hear of a love that is willing to suffer, yea, even to die, in order to win you over?

Jesus demonstrates a love that refuses to give in to vengeance or to give up. He is determined to love the enemy in order to win freedom for them and restore them to the rightful relationship of beloved child and friend. Paul says in Romans 5:8, "God proves his love for us in that while we still were sinners Christ died for us"; and John 3:16 tells us, "For God so loved the world that he gave his only Son, so that everyone who believes in him may not perish but may have eternal life." The cross is the vehicle for demonstrating the full extent of God's love.

—Adam Hamilton, *24 Hours That Changed the World*, page 91

Going Deeper in Truth

Read Isaiah 53:5.

- Christians traditionally identify Jesus as the "suffering servant" whom Isaiah describes in this verse. What does it mean to you that Jesus was "wounded for [your] transgressions" and "crushed for [your] iniquities"? How can you thank Jesus for the sacrifice he made on your behalf?

Read Matthew 25:31-46.

- Jesus doesn't mince words in this message. What does it mean to treat "the least of these" as if they were Jesus himself?

Read Mark 8:34-38.

- What is Jesus talking about when he tells us that, to be his followers, we must "take up [our] cross"? In what ways can we take up our cross?

Experience Life in Community

Help Carry Someone Else's Burden

Simon of Cyrene took on Jesus' burden by carrying his crossbeam to Golgotha. Jesus was undoubtedly weak and dehydrated and unable to carry his cross the entire way himself. Galatians 6:2 instructs Christians to "bear one another's burdens." As a group, plan a project to help people who are carrying a heavy burden. Here are some suggestions:

- Visit an assisted-living facility, and read to or spend time with the residents.

- Organize a canned food drive for hungry people in your community. Work with a local food bank to determine what foods are needed and to promote the drive.
- Write notes of encouragement to your teachers and school administrators.

Spend much time in prayer before making any final decisions about what you will do or the steps you will take. As you plan, consider the following questions:

- Who in our community is carrying a heavy burden?
- What people and groups are already working to ease these burdens? How can we help them?
- How can the members of our group use their unique gifts to serve others?

Making It Personal

Take a vow of "sarcasm sacrifice." Invite your whole group or some of your friends to take it with you. Pray for strength and then do not use sarcasm for the next week. If you do, pause and pray for strength, beginning again.

Closing: Listening for God

As a group, talk about people who are enduring humiliation or who are carrying a heavy burden. This could include people who are bullied, people affected by a natural disaster or epidemic, people persecuted for their faith, public figures involved in scandal, victims of abuse and addiction, and so on. If you have Internet access, look for stories of people who are hurting.

Close in prayer, lifting up all of the groups and individuals you named.

Session 6: The Crucifixion

†

Getting Started

Goals for This Session

—Explore the Gospel accounts of Jesus' crucifixion.

—Understand how Jesus was not only executed but also bullied.

—Understand the significance of the Crucifixion to our salvation.

—Recognize the pain that people experience at the hands of bullies and the extent of the suffering that Jesus experienced on the cross.

Words to Know

Casting lots: tossing stones, sticks, or other objects to make a decision by chance (similar to drawing straws or flipping a coin)

Crucifixion: to put to death by tying or nailing the victim's feet and hands to a cross

Curtain of the Temple: likely refers to the veil covering the "Holy of Holies"—the inner chamber of the Temple that the high priest entered once per year to make atonement for the sins of the people. The curtain being "torn in two, from top to bottom" (Mark 15:38) may represent tearing down the barrier between God and humanity.

Introduction: The Crucifixion and Bullying

✝

Jesus' suffering and death shows us that bullying has been around for a long time. But recent in years, as incidents of bullying and hazing have led to injury and death, the danger of bullying has become a hot topic in the media.

We encounter bullies in just about every television show, book, and movie involving teenagers in a school setting. Some bullies are big and athletic and use their physical strength to push around their smaller peers; some use their popularity as a weapon, threatening to ruin the social lives of anyone who crosses them. These fictional bullies are caricatures, but their real-life counterparts do just as much damage. And the tools that bullies use to cause their victims pain are more numerous than ever. In addition to physical abuse, verbal taunts, and exclusion, today's bullies have access to technology that can instantly spread a hurtful rumor or an embarrassing or compromising photo throughout the entire school (and beyond). They can send intimidating (and sometimes anonymous) text messages or e-mails; they can insult and threaten their victims, without the fear of being overheard by adults.

Bullying—whether physical or emotional, in person or over phones and computers—is responsible for feelings of sadness, alienation, shame, and hopelessness and is responsible for many suicides and violent outbursts. In some cases, the bully is intentionally cruel to his or her victim. In other cases, the bully is not aware of the pain he or she is causing. Many of us are guilty of being bullies. We need to pay attention to how we, through our words and actions, exclude, embarrass, or hurt others (even if we don't mean to).

Jesus was not only executed, he was bullied. We've already seen how he was treated prior to the Crucifixion. Roman soldiers mocked him, sarcastically hailing him as "King of the Jews," dressing him in a royal cloak, and crowning him with thorns. They forced him to carry his crossbeam to the place where he would be killed. And the bullying didn't stop when he was on the cross.

Crucifixion was a public form of execution that was meant to humiliate the person being executed and to intimidate the masses. Jesus was on display for anyone to see. Mark tells us that "Those who passed by derided him" (15:29), making sarcastic remarks about Jesus being the Messiah. The chief priests and scribes, and even those being crucified with Jesus, joined in. The Roman soldiers cast lots, while Jesus was still alive and on the cross, to see who would get his clothing. Meanwhile, Jesus suffered the physical pain of crucifixion. His arms, and possibly his legs, were nailed to the cross. He was hungry and thirsty and naked and likely exhausted from holding up his arms. Jesus spent six hours on the cross before breathing his last. (Some crucifixions took much longer.)

Despite the cruelty and humiliation Jesus experienced on the cross, he died for the bullies that tortured him as much as he died for the few loved ones who stayed with him as he was crucified. He prayed for these bullies: "Father, forgive them; for they do not know what they are doing" (Luke 23:34). He responded with grace, not revenge.

We can learn a great deal from how Jesus responded to bullying. Like Jesus, we should respond with grace, not revenge. (It is important to note that responding with grace does not mean letting oneself be bullied.) And like Jesus, we must be willing to make sacrifices on behalf of others. If a peer is a victim of bullying, we must have the courage to stand up for this person even if it means risking our social standing or making ourselves a target for bullies. Jesus gave everything for us and calls us to give of ourselves for those who need our help.

Biblical Foundation

It was nine o'clock in the morning when they crucified him. The inscription of the charge against him read, "The King of the Jews." And with him they crucified two bandits, one on his right and one on his left. Those who passed by derided him, shaking their heads and saying, "Aha! You who would destroy the temple and build it in three days, save yourself, and come down from the cross!" In the same way the chief priests, along with the scribes, were also mocking him among themselves and saying, "He saved others; he cannot save himself. Let the Messiah, the King of Israel, come down from the cross now, so that we may see and believe." Those who were crucified with him also taunted him.

When it was noon, darkness came over the whole land until three in the afternoon. At three o'clock Jesus cried out with a loud voice, "Eloi, Eloi, lema sabachthani?" which means, "My God, my God, why have you forsaken me?" When some of the bystanders heard it, they said, "Listen, he is calling for Elijah." And someone ran, filled a sponge with sour wine, put it on a stick, and gave it to him to drink, saying, "Wait, let us see whether Elijah will come to take him down." Then Jesus gave a loud cry and breathed his last. And the curtain of the temple was torn in two, from top to bottom. Now when the centurion, who stood facing him, saw that in this way he breathed his last, he said, "Truly this man was God's Son!"—Mark 15:25-39

Video Presentation and Discussion (Optional)

Watch the video segment "The Crucifixion," from the *24 Hours That Changed the World* DVD. (Running Time: 12:54 minutes)

Sights

- The Church of the Holy Sepulcher, the traditional site considered to encompass both the place where Jesus was crucified and the tomb in which he was buried
- The interior of the Chapel of the Crucifixion and the altar that stands over the Rock of Calvary
- A representation of the cross on which Jesus likely was crucified

Key Insights

The Orthodox tradition makes elaborate use of icons of brass; they are a reminder of why most Protestants often find these holy sites overwhelming and ostentatious and why they favor Gordon's Calvary as a place to remember the Crucifixion.

The cross would have been assembled at the site of the Crucifixion. Archaeological evidence indicates that the victims of crucifixion had their feet nailed into the sides of the cross, straddling it. The small ledge was not for the feet but acted as a seat, encouraging the victim to rest upon it, thus pulling at the nails piercing the wrists. Remember, the aim of crucifixion was to inflict as much pain as possible upon the victim for as long as possible.

Roman crosses were six to nine feet high. We tend to imagine Jesus hanging high up; but in reality, Jesus was likely only a foot or so above those who stood around his cross.

- How does this video give you a better idea of how Jesus suffered during the Crucifixion?
- What do we learn from the cross about God's love for us?

63

- What thoughts and/or feelings come to mind when you consider how Jesus suffered on the cross?

Book Study and Discussion (Optional)

Prior to this session, read the sixth chapter (pages 95–113) of *24 Hours That Changed the World*, by Adam Hamilton. Use the following questions to discuss this chapter with your group:

- What did you learn from this chapter about Jesus' crucifixion?
- What made crucifixion such a painful and humiliating form of execution?
- What can we learn from the final words of Jesus recorded in the four Gospels?
- What does this chapter teach us about atonement? How did Jesus, by his death, atone for our sins?

We come now to the cross.

The Romans . . . practiced crucifixion as a means of striking fear in the hearts of the people; and they did so for eight hundred years. It was a terrifying death, and those who witnessed it were not inclined thereafter to violate Roman law. . . . [Roman philosopher] Cicero called crucifixion the "extreme and ultimate punishment of slaves" and the "cruelest and most disgusting penalty." [Ancient Jewish historian] Josephus called it "the most pitiable of deaths."

Crucifixion was an extremely effective crime deterrent, since crucifixions took place along the main thoroughfares where people would see them. . . . Victims were typically left hanging, or their bodies were taken down and left on the ground near the cross until the animals were finished with them.

—Adam Hamilton, *24 Hours That Changed the World*, page 96

Going Deeper in Truth

Read Psalm 22.

- In Matthew and Mark, Jesus' final recorded words before dying are the opening words of this Psalm, "My God, my God, why have you forsaken me?" Christians have long wondered why Jesus, God in human form, felt forsaken on the cross. Long before the Bible had numbered chapters and verses, people referred to a psalm by reciting its first line. Jesus may have been referring to all of Psalm 22 and not just the part about feeling forsaken. What is the overall message of this psalm? How does its tone change as you read from beginning to end?

Read Luke 23:32-43.

- What does it say about Jesus that he could pray and ask forgiveness for the people who were mocking and killing him? What can we learn from Jesus' example?
- What can we learn from Jesus' conversation with the criminal on the other cross about whom Jesus died for and who is welcome in God's kingdom?

Read John 19:26-27.

- Even though Jesus was dying and in agony on the cross, he was concerned about his mother, who was standing close to the cross. He made sure that "the disciple whom he loved" (traditionally identified as John) would take care of her. What does this moment teach us about love?

Read Romans 5:6-11.

- What do Paul's words tell us about Jesus' love for us and about what Jesus did on our behalf? How do these verses put the Crucifixion in perspective?

Experience Life in Community

ACTing Out of Love

Divide participants into small groups of three or four.

Jesus died to make atonement for our sins. Out of love for us, Jesus endured pain, humiliation, and death so that we could be free from sin and death and in a right relationship with God. Jesus calls us to follow his example by giving of ourselves for others. To illustrate this sacrificial love, each group should create a skit in which a character makes a sacrifice out of love for one or more of the other characters.

The groups should spend about five minutes preparing. Then each group should present its skit to the others.

Following the skits, discuss these questions:

- What did you learn from these skits about making sacrifices on behalf of others?
- How did the characters in these skits follow Jesus' example and teaching?
- Where in your life could you make a sacrifice out of love for someone else?
- How could we, as a group, give of our time, talents, and/or possessions to bring healing, relief, joy, or encouragement to others?

I invite you to find yourself in this story. Will you be like the soldiers who cast lots for Jesus' clothing, who missed the power and mystery and wonder of the cross and whose only interest was in a few rags of clothing. . . . Or will you be like the soldier who, having seen all these events that took place in the last hours of Jesus' life, was moved to say, "Truly this man was God's Son?"

—Adam Hamilton, *24 Hours That Changed the World,* page 113

Making It Personal

In the coming week, pay special attention to ways in which you bully or try to embarrass or humiliate others. Think about times when you have spread rumors, excluded peers, made fun of people. Be mindful of insulting things you say or bits of gossip that you pass along in text messages. Keep track of anything you do or are tempted to do that could be considered bullying. Pray each day about the incidents and temptations, asking God for the strength and courage not to participate in bullying. Thank God for Christ, who was bullied and who died for the forgiveness of sins.

Closing: Listening for God

Beforehand, gather several crosses, nails, and artistic depictions of the crucifixion. Arrange these items on a table, or display them throughout your meeting space.

Allow five minutes of silence in which everyone looks at and reflects on these depictions of Jesus' suffering. Then set aside two or three minutes for silent prayer. Participants may choose to say prayers of thanks for what Christ has done on our behalf and may lift up persons today who are victims of humiliation and cruelty. Close this time of silent prayer with a group prayer.

Session 7: Christ the Victor

✝

Getting Started

Goals for This Session
—Explore the Gospel accounts of the hours and days immediately following Jesus' death on the cross, including his burial and resurrection.
—Understand the fear Jesus' followers experienced following his death.
—Understand the eternal significance of the Resurrection.
—Recognize how we can offer the hope of resurrection to a hurting world.

Words to Know
Resurrection: returning to life from death in a physical but completely transformed body
sepulcher: a tomb or place of burial

Introduction: Jesus' Burial and Resurrection and the Day After

†

If it isn't too painful, think back to the worst thing that has happened to you in the past year. Maybe you broke up with a boyfriend or girlfriend or got into a fight with your best friend; maybe you did poorly on an important test; maybe you got into trouble at school and had to face the consequences of your actions. How did you feel?

Now think about how you felt the next day. When you awoke in the morning how long did it take for you to remember what had happened the day before? Was there a moment of peace before your mind filled with bad memories and worries about what was yet to come?

The pain of losing a friend or realizing that you've done something wrong or getting some bad news doesn't just go away. It lingers and feeds emotions such as fear, despair, and anxiety. It causes one to worry about what will happen next and to ask whether things will ever be the same again.

Jesus' disciples knew this feeling. Jesus—their Lord and teacher and leader—had been executed in the most painful and humiliating way possible, and they had betrayed and abandoned him in his most desperate hour. The person whom they had devoted their lives to and called the Messiah was dead. What would they do? What would become of their faith? Would the Roman authorities hunt them down and put them to death too?

A few of Jesus' followers had dared to be present for his burial. Joseph of Arimathea, a wealthy man whom Matthew describes as "a disciple of Jesus" (Matthew 27:57), asked for Jesus' body, prepared it for burial, and placed it in the tomb. But John tells us that even Joseph was a "secret" disciple, who, out of fear, hid his identity as a follower of Christ.

In times of pain and despair, we have trouble moving forward. We would rather withdraw and be alone than to face the challenges that lie ahead. The only way to move on after heartache or tragedy is to have hope. We don't know what gave Jesus' disciples hope in the hours following his death and burial. Maybe they remembered some of the things that Jesus had said about the Son of Man rising again (Mark 9:31) or spending three days in the heart of the earth (Matthew 12:40).

We know that all was not lost for Jesus' followers. After an agonizing Saturday, they awoke Sunday morning to learn that Jesus had risen. The Resurrection was the ultimate reason to be hopeful. Jesus' disciples knew that their Lord was the Messiah, that he had defeated death, and that they could look forward to being resurrected and living eternally with God.

The Resurrection should give us hope as well. The good news that Christ has risen will not make our pain go away or remove all of our fears and worries. But it does give us a reason to keep going. Even in times of fear and pain and anxiety, we can look forward to one day being resurrected with Christ.

Biblical Foundation

When the sabbath was over, Mary Magdalene, and Mary the mother of James, and Salome brought spices so that they might go and anoint him. And very early on the first day of the week, when the sun had risen, they went to the tomb. They had been saying to one another, "Who will roll away the stone for us from the entrance to the tomb?" When they looked up, they saw that the stone, which was very large, had already been rolled back. As they entered the tomb, they saw a young man, dressed in a white robe, sitting on the right side; and they were alarmed. But he said to them, "Do not be alarmed; you are looking for Jesus of Nazareth, who was crucified. He has been raised; he is not here. Look, there is the place they laid him."—Mark 16:1-6

Video Presentation and Discussion (Optional)
Watch the video segment "Christ the Victor," from the *24 Hours That Changed the World* DVD. (Running Time: 11:10 minutes)

Sights
- The soft rock used to carve out tombs
- An actual family tomb with its large round stone rolled to the side
- The Stone of Unction in the Church of the Holy Sepulcher, a stone table representing the place where Jesus' body was prepared for burial
- Also in the center of the Church of the Holy Sepulcher, beneath the Rotunda of the Resurrection, a small shrine called an edicule, which is believed to contain all that remains of the rock tomb of Jesus
- The Garden Tomb, another place believed to have been where Jesus was buried

Key Insights

The practice of using rock burial sites made sense in Palestine because arable (farmable) land was so scarce and the rock beneath the surface was so soft.

The rock tomb in Megiddo is one of the few still in existence and clearly shows how difficult it would have been to roll back the stone once it had been set in place.

The chapel shrine that contains, encased in glass, a small piece of stone believed to be from the tomb of Jesus, is the last Station of the Cross.

Inside the Garden Tomb, you can see that one of the two burial plots is unfinished, leading to speculation that the tomb was never completed after Jesus was resurrected.

John recounts that Jesus was buried and first seen by Mary Magdalene in that garden, clearly alluding to Jesus' restoration of the original garden of Eden.

- How does this video give you a better idea of Jesus' burial and resurrection?
- Think about some of the sites you have seen in the last few videos: Gethsemane, the pit beneath Caiaphas's house, the whipping post, the stone pavement, the Stone of Unction, the Garden Tomb. How has seeing these sites changed the way you understand what Jesus has done for you and what Jesus means to you?

Book Study and Discussion (Optional)

Prior to this session, read the seventh chapter (pages 115–133) of *24 Hours That Changed the World,* by Adam Hamilton. Use the following questions to discuss this chapter with your group:

- What did you learn from this chapter about Jesus' burial and resurrection?

- What, do you think, were Jesus' disciples thinking and feeling on the day following Jesus' death?
- What, do you think, was Jesus doing on the second day? (See *24 Hours That Changed the World,* pages 120–121.)
- Why is the Resurrection so important?

Bringing the Scripture to My Life

- Few of Jesus' followers were present at his burial. One of these followers, Joseph of Arimathea, was afraid to identify himself as one of Jesus' followers. He may have been concerned about his safety or his reputation as a member of the Sanhedrin. When have you been in situations where you kept your identity as a Christian secret out of fear of what other people might think?
- Jesus' disciples were in despair after his death and burial. But Jesus, during his life, had given them hints that he would overcome even death, and this may have given them hope. Where do you find hope during times of despair?
- At first, Jesus' followers had trouble accepting that their Lord had risen. When have you heard news that was so good that you had trouble believing it?
- Jesus' resurrection obviously changed everything for his earliest followers. How has the Resurrection changed your life? How has it changed the world? How can the Resurrection continue changing the world?

It would be difficult to overstate the depths to which the disciples' spirits must have fallen. Fear that they could face Jesus' fate was just part of it. There was also the guilt. They knew Judas was not the only one who had betrayed him. Peter could not shake the moment when his eyes met Jesus' in the courtyard of the high priest after his denial that he even knew him (Luke 22:54-62). The rest had fled in Jesus' hour of need. Only John stood near the cross; the others watched from a distance. None had shown up for Jesus' burial. They felt themselves to be cowards.

Guilt and fear were not all they carried in their hearts that day, however. They had left everything to follow Jesus. They believed that he was the Messiah who would restore Israel. They believed that God was with him in powerful ways and that he had the "words of life." In him they had seen goodness personified. He had shown them love, mercy, and grace. Now the unthinkable had happened. Evil, perpetrated by those who claimed to be righteous, had defeated goodness. Rome's soldiers had defeated God's Messiah. Their King was gone. Their hopes and dreams, even their faith, had been crucified with him; and they must have sunk into utter despair.

—Adam Hamilton, *24 Hours That Changed the World*, pages 118–119

Going Deeper in Truth

Read Jeremiah 32:1-15.

- The people of Judah, much like Jesus' disciples after the Crucifixion, had little reason to hope. Jerusalem was under siege, and both the city and the Temple would soon fall to the Babylonians. Many of the people would be displaced or taken into exile. In this moment of despair and desperation, God asked Jeremiah to buy a piece of property just outside of Jerusalem. Buying property in a land that was about the be conquered made little sense, but it was a sign to the people that "Houses and fields and vineyards shall again be bought in this land" (verse 15). What can you do to bring hope to people during times of despair?

Read Matthew 12:38-40; Mark 9:30-32; and John 2:19-22.

- Jesus didn't keep his resurrection a secret, although some of the things he said about it were probably difficult for his disciples to understand. How might these hints that Jesus left for his disciples have given them hope in the hours following his death and burial?

Read Luke 24:36-43 and John 20:24-29.

- Jesus' disciples were skeptical that their Lord had risen. Why, do you think, were they reluctant to believe the good news that Jesus had returned? How do the disciples' experiences give you hope when you doubt?

Read 1 Corinthians 15:12-19.

- In this Scripture, what does Paul say about the Resurrection? Why is the Resurrection so important to our faith? What is the relationship between Christ's resurrection and the resurrection that we can look forward to?

Experience Life in Community

Share Highs and Lows

Gather into a circle and light a candle. The group should spend a minute or two in silence while each person reflects on the high points and low points of his or her week and how God was present in these moments. Pass the candle around the circle. As each person receives the candle, he or she should tell the group about a high point and a low point during the previous week. He or she should talk about how he or she experienced God's presence both during the high and during the low. If someone isn't comfortable talking about a certain experience, he or she may pass.

When we seek God during our highs and during our lows, we become aware of all the ways that God has blessed us and we remember that God is present with us always. Following this time of highs and lows, read aloud Psalm 139:1-18. Go around the circle, with each person reading a verse.

Making It Personal

Identify one person in your life who is in despair and offer this person a sign of hope. This could involve saying a word of encouragement to a friend who is frustrated and having a bad day or creating and sending a get-well card to someone in the hospital or simply spending time with and listening to someone who is in mourning or is in pain from a broken relationship. You should not minimize the person's problems or tell them that everything will be OK. Rather, you should give them a small reminder that they are loved and that God is still at work in their life.

Closing: Listening for God

As a group, make a list people or communities who are in despair. Include people in your congregation who are dealing with an illness or who have lost a loved one; parts of the world that have been ravaged by war or natural disasters; victims of abuse and addiction; and so on. Lift up in prayer each person and group on your list. As a part of this prayer, spend a few minutes in silence, listening for God and how God might be calling you to bring hope to some of the people and communities you've named.

Continue praying for these people and groups in the coming weeks, always taking time to listen for God and how God calls you to respond to those in despair.

A Churchwide Study of
24 Hours That Changed the World

✝

You Will Need

—a copy of this book for each youth participant and leader

—a copy of *24 Hours That Changed the World*, by Adam Hamilton, for each adult participant (A copy for each youth participant is optional.)

—a copy of the *24 Hours That Changed the World Video Journey* DVD for each adult study group (A copy of the DVD for each youth study group is optional.)

—a copy of *24 Hours That Changed the World for Younger Children* for each leader of children ages 4–8

—a copy of *24 Hours That Changed the World for Older Children* for each leader of children ages 9–12

—a copy of the *24 Hours That Changed the World, 40 Days of Reflection* devotional guide (A copy for every family and/or adult participant is optional.)

Schedule for a Churchwide Study

Many churches have weeknight programs that include an evening meal, an intergenerational gathering time, and separate classes for children, youth, and adults. The following schedule illustrates one way to organize a weeknight program:

- 5:30 P.M.: Gather for a meal.
- 6:00 P.M.: Have an intergenerational gathering that introduces the subject and primary Scripture(s) for that evening's session. (The Scriptures in the children's studies sometimes differ from those in the youth and adult studies.) This time should include appropriate music and an opening prayer or devotion.
- 6:15–7:30 P.M.: Gather in classes for children, youth, and adults.

You may choose to position this study as a Sunday school program. This approach would be similar to the weeknight schedule, except with a shorter class time (which is common for Sunday morning programs):

- Intergenerational gathering, including the reading of the key Scripture(s), an opening prayer or a devotion, and music (*10–15 minutes*)
- Classes for children, youth, and adults (*45 minutes*)

Encourage families and/or individuals to use *24 Hours That Changed the World, 40 Days of Reflection* as a daily devotional guide during the weeks when you do this churchwide, intergenerational study.